The Wild Life of SHARKS

By Camilla de la Bédoyère

WINDMILL BOOKS

THE WILD SIDE

Published in 2015 by **WINDMILL BOOKS**, an Imprint of Rosen Publishing
29 East 21st Street, New York, NY 10010

© 2015 Miles Kelly Publishing

Publishing Director: Belinda Gallagher
Creative Director: Jo Cowan
Editorial Director: Rosie Neave
Designers: Jo Cowan, Venita Kidwai
Image Manager: Liberty Newton
Production Manager: Elizabeth Collins
Reprographics: Stephan Davis, Jennifer Cozens, Thom Allaway

Acknowledgements

The publishers would like to thank Mike Foster (Maltings Partnership), Joe Jones, and Richard Watson (Bright Agency)
for the illustrations they contributed to this book. All other artwork from the Miles Kelly Artwork Bank.

The publishers would like to thank the following sources for the use of their photographs: t = top, b = bottom, l = left,
r = right, c = center, bg = background, rt = repeated throughout. **Cover** (front, m) Visuals Unlimited/Corbis; (back) A Cotton
Photo/Shutterstock; (Speech panel) Tropinina Olga. **Corbis** 1 Visuals Unlimited; 6 Fred Bavendam/Minden Pictures; 14
Douglas P. Wilson/Frank Lane Picture Agency. **FLPA** 7(t) Stephen Belcher/Minden Pictures;18 Norbert Probst/
Imagebroker; 20 Mike Parry/Minden Pictures. **National Geographic Stock** 12–13(m)Brian J. Skerry; 21(b)Paul
Sutherland. **Nature Picture Library** 5(br) Doug Perrine; 11(m) Visuals Unlimited; 15(b) Doug Perrine; 19(t) Bruce
Rasner/Rotman. **Photoshot** 7(b) Oceans Image; 13(t) Oceans Image. **Shutterstock** Repeated throughout: (Header
band) Tyler Fox, ('Learn a word' panel) donatas1205 and artenot, (Speech bubbles) tachyglossus; 2 Sergio Hayashi; 3(t) gfdunt;
4(m) cbpix; 5(tr) Ian Scott; 8('Draw me' heading banner) Ambient Ideas, ('Find out more' panel) Keo/Sergio Hayashi; 8–9(bg)
Liveshot; 9('Shark attack' bg) donatas1205, ('Shark bite' bg) wet nose and Lyolya; 10(m) Specta; 11(b) Ian Scott; 13(b) FAUP;
15(t) Brandelet; 16('How many?' banner) sharpner; 16–17 (bg) Liveshot; 17('Shhhh!' panel) LittleRambo, ('True or false' panel)
Memo Angeles and LittleRambo, ('Whose baby?' panel) M_A_R_G_O; 19(b) Christophe Rouziou; 21(t) Krzysztof Odziomek.

LIBRARY OF CONGRESS CATALOGING-IN-PUBLICATION DATA

De la Bédoyère, Camilla, author.
The wild life of sharks / Camilla de la Bedoyere.
   pages cm. — (The wild side)
 Includes index.
ISBN 978-1-4777-5499-3 (pbk.)
ISBN 978-1-4777-5500-6 (6 pack)
ISBN 978-1-4777-5498-6 (library binding)
1. Sharks—Juvenile literature. I. Title.
QL638.9.D42885 2015
597.3—dc23
                        2014027097

Manufactured in the United States of America

CPSIA Compliance Information: Batch #CW15WM: For Further Information contact Rosen Publishing, New York, New York at 1-800-237-9932

Contents

What are you? 4

What do you eat? 6

 Activity time 8

Where do you live? 10

How fast do you swim? 12

What are your babies called? 14

 Puzzle time 16

What do you look like? 18

Are you scary? 20

 Old Shark's Birthday 22

Glossary, Index, and Websites 24

What are you?

I am a shark!

Sharks are fish. We are super swimmers. Gills allow us to breathe underwater.

Dorsal fin

Gill slits

Mouth

Q. Why are fish so smart?

A. Because they live in schools!

Pectoral fin

4

Some sharks are no bigger than your hand!

LEARN A WORD:

gills

Fish do not have lungs. They breathe with gills instead.

Tail fin

Meet my family

Sharks belong to the same fish family as rays and skates.

Ray

Rays have flat bodies and some "fly" through the sea.

Skate

Skates have flat bodies and swim near the seabed.

5

What do you eat?

Fish

I eat other animals.

Most sharks feed on squid, fish, and small sea creatures. Some even eat other sharks!

Q. What does a shark eat for lunch?

A. Peanut butter and jellyfish sandwich!

6

Giant leap

Great white sharks eat seals. They leap out of the water to grab them.

Seals

Open wide

Basking sharks feed on tiny creatures called plankton. They swim with their mouths open to catch them.

Plankton

7

Activity time

Get ready to make and do!

Find out more

Sharks grow new teeth all the time, but you will only have two sets. Find out how many teeth you have now, and how many you will have when you are an adult.

Draw me!

YOU WILL NEED: pencils · paper

1. Draw a long semicircle. Add triangles for the fins and tail.

3. Add the nostril, teeth, and gills. Shape the nose and fins.

2. Shape the body. Draw the eye, mouth, and extra fins.

Now color me in and give me a name!

8

Shark attack!

Ask for help!

YOU WILL NEED:
paper and pens · string
chopsticks · small magnets
scissors · paper clips

HERE'S HOW:
1. Draw and cut out lots of small fish.
2. Attach a paper clip to each one.
3. For each fishing rod, tie one end of a piece of string to the end of a chopstick. Tie a magnet to the loose end of the string.
4. To play, scatter the fish on the floor and use your rods to pick them up.

Shark bite!

Ask for help!

YOU WILL NEED:
bread · your favorite
sandwich filling · knife
blueberries · slice of cheese
1 chocolate chip or raisin

HERE'S HOW:
1. Make your favorite sandwich.
2. Cut it into a shark shape, with fins and a tail.
3. Put your shark on a plate.
4. Place blueberries around the shark to create the sea.
5. Cut the cheese "teeth" and put in place.
6. Use a chocolate chip or raisin for the eye.

9

Where do you live?

Reef shark

I live on coral reefs.

There are lots of other animals here. I can always find plenty of food.

Q. Why do sharks swim in salt water?

A. Because pepper makes them sneeze!

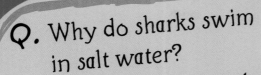

On the move

Blue sharks do not live in one place. They swim through the world's seas, looking for food and mates.

Blue shark

River swimmer

Most sharks live in the sea, but bull sharks often swim into rivers.

Bull shark

11

How fast do you swim?

I am super speedy.

I am a mako, the fastest shark in the world.

Q. Where should you go to escape from a bad-tempered shark?

A. As far away as possible!

Mako shark

12

Greenland shark

Slowly does it
Greenland sharks live in the cold seas of the north. Most of them are blind, and they swim at a slow pace.

Hitch a ride!
Sharksuckers are fish that hold on to sharks. As the sharks swim, they are taken along for the ride!

13

What are your babies called?

My babies are called pups.

Some sharks lay eggs. An embryo grows inside each egg.

Laying eggs

Shark ·········· embryo

LEARN A WORD:
embryo
A baby that is growing inside an egg, or its mother.

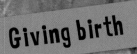

Get together
In the spring, lots of hammerheads meet in the same part of the sea. They will mate here.

Giving birth
Not all sharks lay eggs. Some of them give birth to their pups.

Q. What is a shark's favorite day?
A. Chewsday!

Giving birth

15

Puzzle time

Can you solve all the puzzles?

Start here

Lost teeth

Can you help Sally the shark find her way out of the coral maze?

How many?

Can you add these up?

ANSWERS: 1. 5 2. 5 3. 5

1.

2.

3.

16

True or false?

1. All sharks are fish.
2. Sharks breathe using lungs.
3. A hammerhead is a type of shark.

ANSWERS: 1. True 2. False 3. True

Shhhh!

The word "shark" begins with the sound "sh." Each of these words also has the sound "sh." Can you figure out what they are?

_ _oe = shoe

_ _ip
squa_ _
wa_ _
spla_ _
fi_ _
_ _ell

ANSWERS: 1. ship 2. squash 3. wash 4. splash 5. fish 6. shell

Whose baby?

Can you match the animal parent to its baby?

Shark	Calf
Elephant	Pup
Horse	Chick
Pig	Piglet
Bird	Foal

ANSWERS:
Shark — Pup
Elephant — Calf
Horse — Foal
Pig — Piglet
Bird — Chick

17

What do you look like?

I look strange!

I am a hammerhead shark. My strange head helps me to see well, and to find my prey. I eat fish, squid, and stingrays.

One eye at each end of the "hammer"

Scalloped hammerhead

Big mouth

The megamouth shark has a huge mouth. During the day, it swims in the deep, dark part of the sea.

Megamouth

Q. Have you ever seen a shark cry?

A. No, but I have seen a whale blubber!

Covered in spots

Sharks have rough, tough skin. Some sharks have plain skin, and some have spots or stripes.

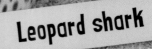

Leopard shark

19

Are you scary?

I am not as scary as I look!

Sharks like eating fish, not people. We like to be left alone in our ocean home.

Great white shark

20

Gentle giant

Whale sharks are the biggest fish in the world. They are very friendly, and divers like to swim with them.

Whale shark

Sharks need help

Scientists look after sharks. They count them and measure them. Scientists want to help sharks survive.

Q. How do you take a shark's temperature?

A. Very carefully!

21

Old Shark's Birthday

Old Shark was so old he did not know his birthday – he had never had a birthday cake or presents.

Crab and Octopus thought this was sad. They decided to throw a surprise party for him and started planning.

On Sunday, they ordered Old Shark's favorite foods – shellfish sandwiches, jellyfish and ice cream, and a fishcake with candles.

On Monday, Octopus organized all the decorations. He bought party hats, balloons, and a banner that said "Happy Birthday Old Shark!."

On Tuesday, Crab booked Old Shark's favorite rock band, The Jaws, to play at the party.

On Wednesday, Octopus booked Coral the Clownfish as an entertainer. "She sounds shrimply wonderful!" said Crab.

On Thursday the friends bought Old Shark's presents. They got him a toothbrush and a fishing rod.

22

On Friday the two were congratulating themselves on doing such a great job. Suddenly Crab turned pale. "Oh no!" he said. "We forgot to send invitations!"

Quick as a flash, Octopus wrote a sea-mail to every shark in the ocean, asking them to come to Old Shark's surprise birthday party the next day.

On Saturday morning, Crab and Octopus went to see Old Shark. They told him that they had decided that today was his birthday. Old Shark was surprised and pleased to see the wonderful party that they had organized for him, with the food, the presents, and the decorations.

Just then, the guests began to arrive – and they were looking hungry! There was Great White, Hammerhead, Lemon, Bull, and Tiger. "Time for us to go now!" said Octopus and Crab, and they made a quick getaway.

By Camilla de la Bédoyère

23

Glossary

banner a long sign, often made of cloth

dorsal on the upper side or back of an animal

pectoral on the chest

plankton a tiny plant or animal that floats in the ocean

pup a baby shark

ray a broad, flat marine or freshwater fish

scatter spread in various random directions

skate large marine fish of the ray family that swims at the bottom of the ocean

Websites

For web resources related to the subject of this book, go to: **www.windmillbooks.com/weblinks** and select this book's title.